BANTER

BANTER

Oodles of Love

Nathan Minnehan

Walkntalk Publishing, Chicago.

BANTER
Oodles of Love

By Nathan Minnehan

ISBN: **979-8-9949706-4-5**

Published by:

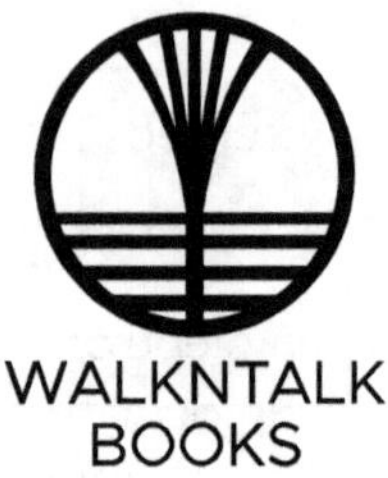

An imprint of:

WalknTalk Books

7100 N Sheridan Rd

Chicago, IL 60626

Table of Contents

Banter

The Playful and friendly exchange of teasing remarks.

(Google :-)

"Moments without words are letters without lines to write them on ... almost lost, but somehow rescued by someone dumb enough to write them down!"

-Nathan Minnehan, BANTER

PRE-BANTER

"The Place Where Minnehan BANTER Flourished"

By Nathan Minnehan, author of STITCH

I remember the light that used to shine through her eyes when she cupped her hand under her chin, smiled and said "how are you doll?" Her infectious laughter that soared over every television set in the house as she carried on chatting over the phone with friends, family, and relatives from around the country. I remember the musty smell of her lovely home covered in flower patterns, porcelain frogs with hats on them, and pictures of grandchildren scattered along every dresser, end table, and railing. I remember the sound of the birds chirping and the storm door closing as I'd step outside her back porch. I remember the sound of sticks braking under my golf spikes as I walked through her imperfect yard, and around the fence where I got forty-five stitches from climbing when I was five. I remember the slow putting green just outside her kitchen window where my brother and I used to practice until dark. I remember stealing silver half dollars from a sippy cup in Papa's room to pay for rounds of golf on the par three golf course past the fence and next to the putting green. I remember the quiet sound of a track of holes that teleported you into another time period, decade, and place in time. I remember my brother's story of his first hole in one on the course. I remember crab apple wars outside her backyard with our cousins from Michigan. I remember sleepovers with twenty or more cousins, aunts and uncles piled all into one house.

I remember an old tv playing MTV hits in the family room, and my cousin running up the stairs to hear Mo Money Mo Problems by The Notorious B.I.G. I remember playing basketball in the cul-de-sac, and days when the sun heated the driveway in an attempt to singe the skin off of my feet. I remember the acorns in her front yard, and Papa's green garbage cans used to pick up the sticks off of "the front, side, and back lawn." I remember the squirrel traps, and Papa sitting on the front porch smoking Pall Malls and flicking my ear lobes to make sure I was still awake.⊠ I remember the tight squeeze the door made when it shut and the sound of warmth, family, and Minnehan's inside. I remember all of this, and what's more, I remember the ways they said the things they did. And by a long shot, I am more grateful now that I can share them with you.

Hopefully these words will inspire you to share your family magic with the world as well.

Mimi's Adages...

"As you wander through life, whatever be your goal, keep your eye upon the doughnut and not upon the hole"

-Mimi

“I’m off like a dirty old sock”

-Mimi

“There is enough food for Cox’s army”

-Mimi

“you’re slower than molasses in January”

-Mimi

“Don’t trouble trouble until trouble troubles you”

-Mimi

“It’s better to be ready and not go than to go and not be ready”

-Aunt Margaret and Mimi

"...Your faith will see you through, you know, I am living testimony of it."

-Mimi

“There’s only one way to do things, and that’s the right way”

-Mimi

“Heavens to murgatroyd”

-Mimi

“You’d lose your head if it wasn’t attached”

-Mimi

“Your father could work all day in a two court pail, and not get anything done”

“I’m under the alcho-flu-ence of incohol like some leeple pink I am!”

-Mimi

“You’ll be dead in the morning”

-Mimi

“God bless the potatoes and God bless the meat. Everybody that’s hungry, pitch in and eat!”

-Mimi

“Ockle doockle” -Mimi

“Can you crack a louse on your tummy?”

-Mimi

Mimi's Toasts...

“Okay let’s all belly up to the bar now”

-Mimi

"Here's to life, and ain't it grand? I just got a divorce from my old man. And here's to the judge, and his grand decision. He gave the kids to my husband, and they ain't even his-in"

-Mimi

"It's five o'clock somewhere, make me a manny"

-Mimi

“Here’s to a moment of great repose. It’s tummy to tummy and toes to toes. One mom- ent of sheer delight, and it’s fanny to fanny the rest of the night”

-Mimi

Papa's Adages...

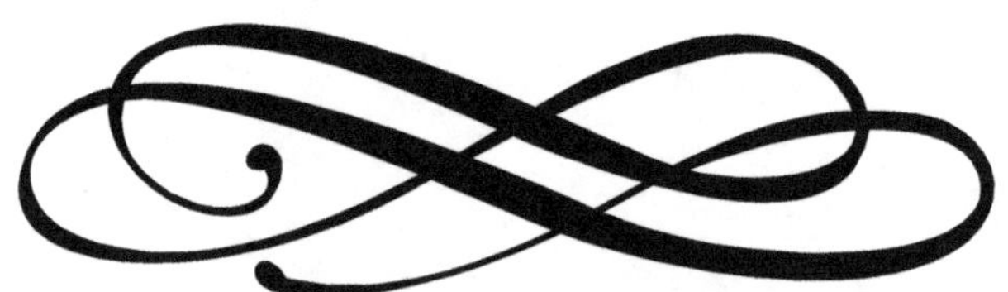

“Blow it out your barracks bag Johnny”

-Papa

“For God’s sake, whatever you do, keep your pecker in your pants”

-Papa

“Go piss up a rope, and watch it shrink”

-Papa

“They don’t know their assholes from a hole in the ground”

-Papa

“When pigs fly”

-Papa

“A pig’s ass you will...”

-Papa

“why don’t you do me a favor and pick up the sticks along the front, side, and back yard?”

-Papa

“You’re about as useful as tits on a boar hog”

-Papa

"Bend over so I can shove my size ten triple E up your ass"

-Papa

“Straighten up and fly right”

-Papa

“Hope to shit in your mess kit”

-Papa

Poems she knew by heart

• • •

IF *by Rudyard Kipling*

If you can keep your head when all about you
Are losing theirs and blaming it on you,
If you can trust yourself when all men doubt you,
But make allowance for their doubting too;
If you can wait and not be tired by waiting,
Or being lied about, don't deal in lies, Or being hated, don't give way to hating,
And yet don't look too good, nor talk too wise:
If you can dream and not make dreams your master;
If you can think and not make thoughts your aim;
If you can meet with Triumph and Disaster
And treat those two impostors just the same;
If you can bear to hear the truth you've spoken
Twisted by knaves to make a trap for fools,
Or watch the things you gave your life to, broken,
And stoop and build 'em up with worn-out tools:
If you can make one heap of all your winnings
And risk it on one turn of pitch-and-toss, And lose, and start again at your beginnings And never breathe a word about your loss;

If you can force your heart and nerve and sinew
To serve your turn long after they are gone,
And so hold on when there is nothing in you Except
the Will which says to them: 'Hold on!'
If you can talk with crowds and keep your virtue,
Or walk with Kings nor lose the common touch,
If neither foes nor loving friends can hurt you,
If all men count with you, but none too much; If
you can fill the unforgiving minute
With sixty seconds' worth of distance run,
Yours is the Earth and everything that's in it, And
which is more you'll be a Man, my son!

Don't Quit *This poem was found on Unlce Otto Cuyler's letterhead and signed*
- THE KINGFISH

When things go wrong, as they sometimes will,
When the road you're trudging seems all uphill,
When the funds are low and the debts are high, And you want to smile, but you have to sigh, When care is pressing you down a bit-
Rest if you must, but don't you quit.
Life is queer with its twists and turns,
As every one of us sometimes learns,
And many a fellow turns about
When he might have won had he stuck it out. Don't give up though the pace seems slow You may succeed with another blow.
Often the goal is nearer than It seems to a faint and faltering man;
Often the struggler has given up
When he might have captured the victor's cup; And he learned too late when the night came down,
How close he was to the golden crown.

Success is failure turned inside out -
The silver tint in the clouds of doubt,
And you never can tell how close you are,
It might be near when it seems afar;
So stick to the fight when you're hardest hit
-It's when things seem worst that you must not quit.

To My Mother *a prayer written for Mary Ann's father, Charles Murphy*

To My Mother

Dear God, wilt Thou a message
take
For one who walks the golden
way?
She is my own, my very own.
Without her all are empty day
Whisper that my heart is with
her
In that kingdom up above
Tell her that I miss her
always
And I send her all my love.
Dear God, you will know my
mother
By the beauty of her smile
Wilt Thou say to her I'm
coming
Home in just a little while.

BR-1938

"Your faith will see you through. You know, I am a living testimony of it." Time sometimes just can't break the bonds of sadness, and as Maryann recited from heart word for word a prayer that she heard only once at her father's funeral, I realized something. Sadness gains an element of beauty as time goes on. She struggled through a heart-throbbing prayer that was written for her father by his secretary's aunt, a nun, who had been told of how he adored his mother so.

-Mimi's Oral History

Rig a Jig Jig *By Nathan Minnehan and Great-Grandfather Charles Murphy*

Capo 4

C F

Kids get in the car now

C G

It's time to go away so far now

C F

Kids say good bye to Grandma

C G

We're leaving Grandma's house today

Terry and Eddie in the back now Michael in the back window

Tom's on the floor, against the door Waiting for somebody to wake him up

F C G

ooo a rig a jig jig, and away we go

C F

away we go, away we go

C G

a rig a jig jig and away we go

C F C

hi ho, hi ho, hi ho...-Mimi's Oral History

Over the hills, and threw the woods
And into town they drove
And up and down they bounced around
As Papa drove them home
Ooo a rig a jig jig, and away we go
Away we go, away we go
A rig a jig jig, and a way we go
hi ho, hi ho, hi ho...
Then in flash, they were back
And told to go to bed
But the kids all stared at the top of the stairs
As they asked for one more song...
Ooo a rig a jig jig, and away we go
Away we go, away we go
A rig a jig jig, and away we go
hi ho, hi ho, hi ho...

"Mary Ann has Faith, for she knows her well"

Oral History by Nathan Minnehan

At seven o'clock a noisy dinner party had rushed into Duffy's sports bar for the two for one special, known as the "twofer," on wine, beer, and well drinks, in Stuart Florida. It was a chilly night about sixty-five degrees. Mimi, and I decided to say grace. We looked at each other from across the table, and she began the prayer. "Dear God thank you for my beautiful grandchildren, keep them well, healthy and safe. Thank you for the rest of my family, who are my whole life, and lets hope that Papa's looking after us." And just as she finished, her voice ran up, and a twinkle came to the corner of her eye. Eighty-years-old, and vibrant still, her spunky sweetness emanates from roots that reach down beyond what I ever knew of her fascinating past. Her father was defense attorney during prohibition, and defended the bootleggers. His name was Charles Walter Murphy, a jovial character, the youngest of twelve children, and the only one to go to college in his family.

He was a gregarious man, known for hosting parties in his basement for his friends and clients. The basement was lined with paintings from a local Livonia, New York artist named Al Davis. The cellar windows were covered with velvet drapes, and two slot machines hid inside disguised flour bins. "The cupboards were built in, and the handles were at the top," said Mary Ann. Mary Ann and her sister Ginger, two years older, would get quarters from their father, and the two would horse around on the machines. They weren't allowed downstairs during the parties, but Mary Ann recalls the traveling sound of her mother's voice. "They would serve booze to their friends, and my mother would play the ukulele and sing," she said. The only song she could recall was a 1919 special by Albert Campbell and Irving Gllette called "I'm forever blowing bubbles."

Mary Ann's parents were wealthy.

"They lived the good life by every standard, big cars, big trips, and big vacations," as she put it. But when Charles got sick, a harsh reality crippled the family. "We were considered wealthy, and all of the sudden, nothing," said Mary Ann. Exorbitant hospital bills "ate up all the money," and the girls' mother Virginia Murphy soon became completely incapable of caring for them due to a severe drinking problem. Before becoming foster children, Mary Ann and her sister Ginger, nine and eleven-years-old, were scooped up by their Aunt Margaret, a 60-year-old maiden. "She'd never been married, never had any children, and at age 60 she took it upon herself to raise two children," said Mary Ann, still baffled by her courage. When she and her sister Ginger moved in with Aunt Margaret, the state was obliged to check on the children's living quarters, and dwelling environment at their new home.

"They were skeptical of this 60-year-old lady being able to do the job," said Mary Ann. So Aunt Margaret had the girls dressed in pretty patent leather shoes and nice dresses, and a week after the visit, a check arrived in the mail. "And not only that, I love this part of that story," she said, "We qualified as what they called 'welfare children' then," and so "we qualified for welfare payments." A check arrived a week after the foster agency came. "Aunt Margaret wrote a note and put [the check] back in the envelope," saying "Charlie Murphy's children will not be raised on welfare money, do not send anymore checks." Her Aunt Margaret felt the children were "above that," and that she could "scrimp and save," and work hard to support them without taking public money. She reflected back on this moment with a serious tone, and made an aside. "I could tell you now at 80, and I'm sincere about this, If I couldn't take care of myself with my own finances that are coming in, don't tell me that I couldn't get a job, because I could, and I would, and I still maintain that. It's just a pride thing, and there's quite a bit of Irish in it if you'd like to know," she said with a long smirk running across her face.

The voice of seagulls rang all around, and the sea glistened from sunlight that shone like emeralds upon the horizon. The day's weather resembled the seamless view of the skyline on the western New York farm where she took her first employment at age 13. An old truck with wooden slats encasing the bed drove around to pick up all the children set to work that summer time. They worked from eight A.M. to noon, four days a week, weeding beets, picking beans, and picking up potatoes. Mary Ann absolutely dreaded putting her hands in the dirt, but Ginger her sister was a "pro." The two of them worked side by side along with Mary Ann's best friend Midge making five cents for every bushel of potatoes. She claimed that the two of them were so good to her that they would see her lagging behind, and she would toss potatoes into her basket because Mary Ann had such an awful look on her face.

She wasn't incredibly big in size or stature, and because of this, she evaded a few responsibilities along the way.

Mary Ann and her sister Ginger cultivated a fine relationship growing up. "I used to read. Read all the time," and when it was time to do the dishes, "my aunt would say "leave her alone, she likes to read, and my sister would get stuck with all the work." "I feel guilty about it now," she admits, "but I loved to read, and it sure was a good remedy, better than the dishes, for sure." She continued talking about how she and Ginger were in many ways just about polar opposites. "I wouldn't do anything that I was told not to do, and she would do just about everything that she was told not to do. My sister Ginger would swear me to secrecy, and climb out the window, and go to a bar with an older guy. And I never had the nerve to do those kinds of things, plus I didn't really want to. I just didn't want to risk it, you know?" In light of this, dating Donald Beecher in high school seemed to be proof of how she "played it safe." "The big thing about Donald Beecher was you knew that he wasn't going to try to you know what, and his mother had a brand new Mercury," said Mary Ann. "He was not good-looking and not considered flattering for anybody to go out with, but he was safe okay," she cracked up. She thoroughly relished in the nice places that he dined her in, hanging on to every note of some of the good singers on stage. "But I had kind of an ulterior motive because he knew that I wanted to get my driver's license, and he knew that we didn't have a car," said Mary Ann. Donald's mother was class-mates with Charles Murphy, Mary Ann's deceased father, and because she was so fond of him in high school, she let Donald teach her to drive on her brand new Mercury.

"I'll never forget taking the driver's test over in Geneseo," she mentioned. She had passed it the first time, but not without her Irish luck to pull her through a questionable portion of the exam. When told to parallel park, "I pulled up right parallel with the car and he said okay, now parallel park," she laughed and said "I am, and he passed me anyway!"

Mary Ann fondly remembers going to school in the small town of Livonia, New York. She was heavily involved in school operettas such as Pirates of Penzance and H.M.S. Pinafore, in which she had the lead playing Little Buttercup. "Oh I loved doing that stuff Oh God!" she gasped. She remembers her music teacher, Ms. Sands, who had been a victim of Polio, and had to wear braces around her legs, which made you wonder "how she ever did what she did." Mary Ann would wait at Ms. Sands door sobbing with a problem that only Ms. Sands could resolve. "I'll never forget her, she was my everything," said Mary Ann. One story came to mind about Ms. Sands that Mary Ann said she still thinks on with disbelief. "This one week we all had to prepare a song for and sing a solo, and I chose the Shubrick's Our Father. I got up there and I couldn't even start the thing, I just went all to pieces," she said. "And so the next day, she said okay Mary Ann, put your face to the blackboard and sing. I sang the Our Father and do you know everybody clapped; I could have died. Everybody was like who did that come out of, I guess I wondered too, you know."

The seagulls still sang out, but now more noticeably present were the sandpipers that walked near to us. Mary Ann paused for a moment, and then proceeded to endow me with a sliver of her wisdom. "You have people along the way always that other people wouldn't know that make a tremendous impact upon your life." "It seems like a whole lot of people, but out of that it seems like a handful of people that really make a difference in your life. She was that person for me." She reminisced of a moment that came later in her professional life. She was on a business call, and out by

Ms. Sands, who she learned had become quite ill, and thought she'd pay her a visit.

"She was wrapped in a blanket in her chair you know, and she said to me 'Mary Ann, don't forget your talent, use it.' I thought what talent, you know? The only talent I had I used after that to go on and have six children and seventeen grandchildren."

She then proceeded to tell me about when she was married with two kids, and only 22-years-old, when she received a heart wrenching phone call from her sister Ginger's husband ten days before Ginger passed away. She had been suffering from Acute Neufritis, a kidney disease, and suddenly was deathly ill. Mary Ann and her husband Jerry flew to New Jersey to be with her. A little over a week later, her sister was dead. "I slept with her the night she died you know." Mary Ann was 22-years-old. Her father and sister had died, and her mother was absent from her life since Aunt Margaret had taken custody of her and her sister.

She turned and said something that still sticks with me. "Your faith will see you through. You know, I am a living testimony of it."

Time sometimes just can't break the bonds of sadness, and as Mary Ann recited from heart word for word a prayer that she heard only once at her father's funeral, I realized some-thing. Sadness gains an element of beauty as time goes on. She struggled through a heart-throbbing prayer that was written for her father by his secretary's aunt, a nun, who had been told of how he adored his mother so.

Dear God, wilt Thou a message take
For one who walks the golden way?
She is my own, my very own.
Without her all are empty day.
Whisper that my heart is with her
In that kingdom up above
Tell her that I miss her always
And I send her all my love.

Dear God, you will know my mother
By the beauty of her smile
Wilt Thou say to her I'm coming
Home in just a little while.

Maryann smiled and said "boy you're taking me back in time. Holy smokeys."

BANTER NOTES

BANTER NOTES

BANTER NOTES

BANTER NOTES

BANTER NOTES

BANTER NOTES

BANTER NOTES

BANTER NOTES

BANTER NOTES

BANTER NOTES

BANTER NOTES

BANTER NOTES

BANTER NOTES

BANTER NOTES

BANTER NOTES

BANTER NOTES

BANTER NOTES

BANTER NOTES

BANTER NOTES

BANTER NOTES

BANTER NOTES

BANTER NOTES

BANTER NOTES

BANTER NOTES

BANTER NOTES

BANTER NOTES

BANTER NOTES

BANTER NOTES

BANTER NOTES

BANTER NOTES

BANTER NOTES

BANTER NOTES

BANTER NOTES

BANTER NOTES

BANTER NOTES

BANTER NOTES

BANTER NOTES

BANTER NOTES

BANTER NOTES

BANTER NOTES

BANTER NOTES

BANTER NOTES

BANTER NOTES

BANTER NOTES

BANTER NOTES

BANTER NOTES

BANTER NOTES

BANTER NOTES

BANTER NOTES

BANTER NOTES

BANTER NOTES

BANTER NOTES

BANTER NOTES

BANTER NOTES

BANTER NOTES

BANTER NOTES

BANTER NOTES

BANTER NOTES

BANTER NOTES

BANTER NOTES

BANTER NOTES

BANTER NOTES

BANTER NOTES

BANTER NOTES

BANTER NOTES

BANTER NOTES

BANTER NOTES

BANTER NOTES

BANTER NOTES

BANTER NOTES

BANTER NOTES

BANTER NOTES

BANTER NOTES

BANTER NOTES

BANTER NOTES

BANTER NOTES

BANTER NOTES

BANTER NOTES

BANTER NOTES

BANTER NOTES

BANTER NOTES

BANTER NOTES

BANTER NOTES

BANTER NOTES

BANTER NOTES

BANTER NOTES

BANTER NOTES

BANTER NOTES

BANTER NOTES

BANTER NOTES

BANTER NOTES

BANTER NOTES

BANTER NOTES

About the Author

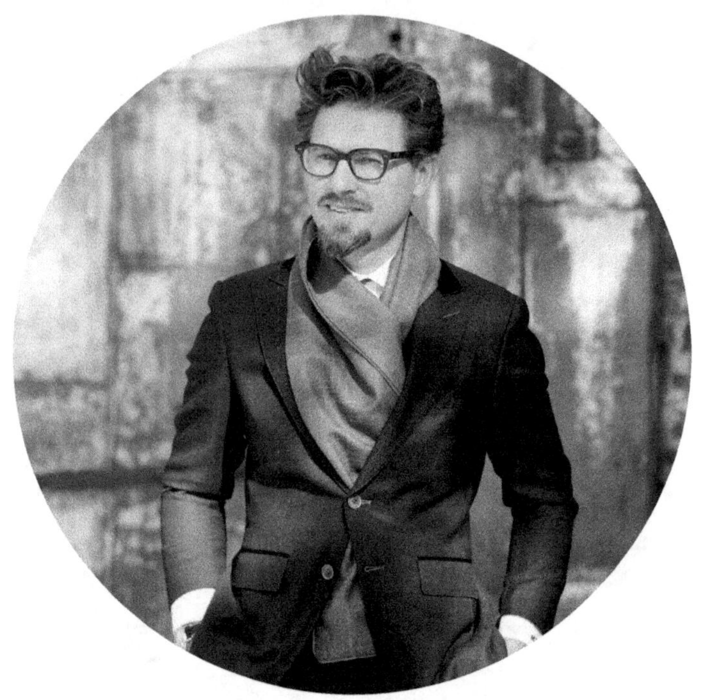

Nathan Minnehan

Inspired by the words of his grandmother Mary Ann "Mimi", Nathan was later inspired to launch a men's suits and leather goods brand called Big Murphy's based on Mary Ann's father, Charlie Murphy, "Big Murphy."

Learn more about the brand at

www.bigmurphys.com, and find other books by

Nathan at

www.nathan.life

Other books by this author...
Available at www.nathan.life

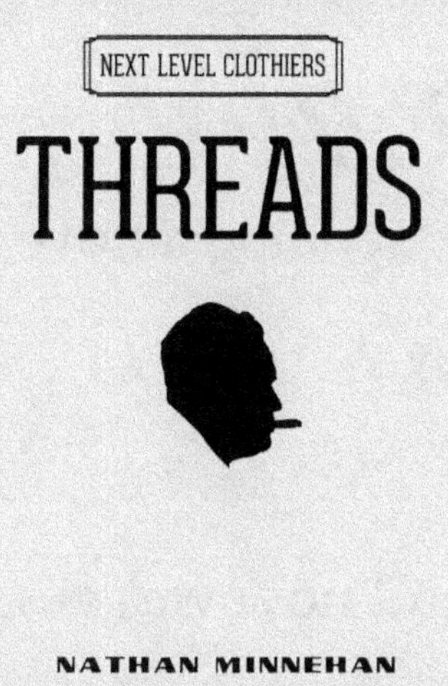

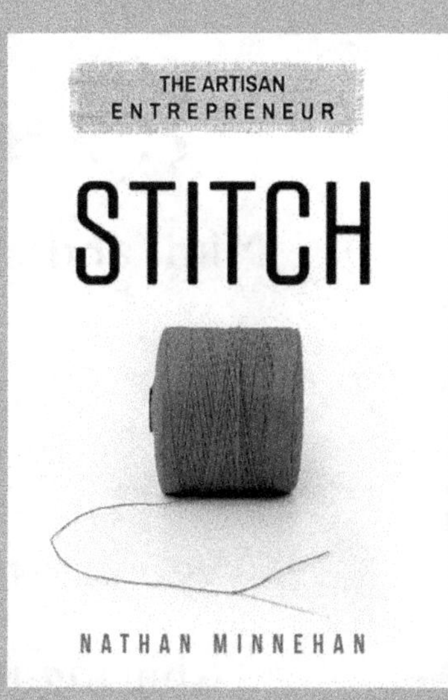

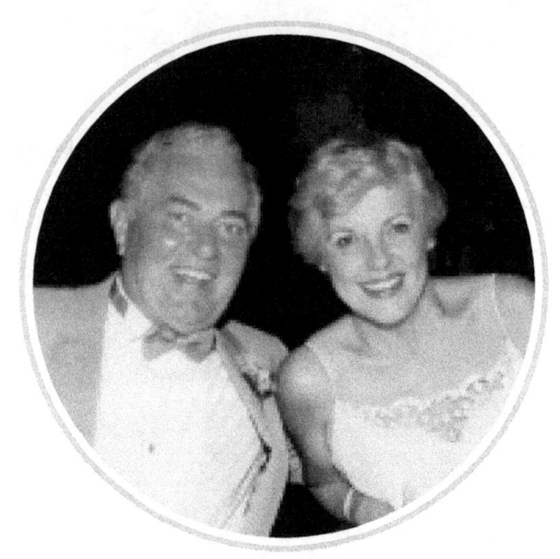

Thank you

Mimi and Papa for sending all of your love!

We received it, and now we're sharing it with the world...

www.ingramcontent.com/pod-product-compliance
Lightning Source LLC
LaVergne TN
LVHW010917110826
845149LV00013B/2397